THE ULTIMATE SNEAKER BOOK FOR **SNEAKERHEADS**

SNEAKER
MAYHEM
2022

GOLDEN LION
PUBLICATIONS

ISBN: 9798750414017

GIVEAWAY

WIN IN TWO EASY STEPS

1
SCAN
**THE QR CODE
LOCATED AT THE
LAST PAGE OF THE BOOK**

2
FOLLOW
**THE
GOLDEN LION PUBLICATIONS
INSTAGRAM PAGE**

WIN A PAIR OF
NIKE AIR FORCE 1

WINNER WILL BE ANOUNCED ON THE 29TH JANUARY 2022

INTRODUCTION

Sneakers can tell you a lot about a person, and Sneaker Mayhem 2022 can tell you a lot about sneakers. Specifically, this year's hottest new releases. In this book, you will find all of the top brands' new sneaker lines that have dropped during 2021 is over. We will take a look at new sneakers from Nike, Adidas, New Balance and more as we trek through these pages. Don't think of this as just a catalog though, for there is so much more in store for you as you read.

Many designs have been released this year, and so many shoes to choose from. In 2021, Nike and Adidas are releasing multiple new designs, we have a company starting their own sneaker line this year, and of course the family favorites, New Balance and Reebok are coming in hot as well with some new stuff for us.

Sneaker Mayhem 2022 will guide you through all of the sneaker releases we had this year by your favorite brands, and allow you to bask in your inner sneaker fantasies.

Along with all of these details, you will also find that the pages are filled with history of different sneaker lines, so that even beginner sneakerheads can find some interesting knowledge about their newfound passion. Sure, you don't need to know everything about something to love it, but the more you know, the more there is to love.

If you want to learn about sneakers, and be up to date on the current releases, then you are in the right place. This is more than just a catalog of everything that has been released in 2021, this is a manual to help even newbies be informed. History meets the present in this book, because sneakers are created for more than just walking.

Sneakers don't just cover your feet, they can also make a statement. A pair bought from a collaboration where the proceeds go to charity show the giving nature of the person. High profile shoes can show that someone is interested in fashion, or just wants to be set apart from the crowd. Simple, yet clean shoes can show that a person can mix business with style. There are so many things we can learn about a person by the shoes they wear and collect, what shoes will you choose from this year's releases? Well, first you need to know what they are. So let's get to it, shall we?

Nike SB Dunk Low 'Street Hawker'

$580

Have you ever been to a street market in another country? China has some of the nicest food vendors in the world. They are everywhere. Street markets are part of the economy and a good chunk of the aesthetic there.

The Street Hawkers are a gently priced pair of sneakers that pay homage to the street food vendors of China.

So what is so special about these sneakers? Well, besides their inspiration being so down to earth, the shoes are two different color schemes! No, they aren't mismatched as the different colors complement each other nicely, but they are not identical patterns like you would find on most sneakers. While the colors of the left shoe mimic three popular dishes in China, the colors of the right shoe represent the different flavor profiles from sweet to spicy.

The left shoe also has a wood grain swoosh in honor of the common use of chopsticks in Chinese culture, and the right shoe has a silver swoosh to resemble the meat hook used to hang roast goose (a very popular dish in the culture). These shoes retailed at $110.

Nike SB Dunk Low Pro 'Parra Abstract Art'

$390

Parra is a Dutch artist, who originates in Amsterdam. His real name is Pieter Janssen, and he started out with designing flyers for music venues, and now he is considered a fine art artist. His works are compared to those of Moscoso and Haring, as he has a post pop vibe with a curve towards the abstract. He has a very unique and distinguished style, and has since teamed up to use that style on some Nike kicks.

Designed by the Dutch artist, these shoes are similar to the ones that the artist created with Nike for the Olympics. Created with skateboarders in mind, these low profile Dunks will rock your world when you first see them. With a typical white base color, things don't stay typical. They aren't dubbed "Abstract Art" for no reason.

The heel, heel tab, eyestays, mudguard, and tongue trim are filled with vibrant, bold colors and wavy designs. The Nike swoosh is found in its typical spot, but also on the toe of the shoe as well. Simple black for the big swoosh, and white for the toe swish avoid drawing attention to the bold colors around them. Parra's logo is found on the back of these beautiful shoes as well.

These sneakers retailed at $110.00.

Nike Dunk Low
'Retro White Black'

$390

These sleek black and white basketball style kicks are sure to bring a hint of nostalgia when you slip them on. Their two tone design features an all-over sleek white finish with black leather accents. The tongue displays a mesh-like material, and the dark laces contrast beautifully with the white of the shoe.

These shoes give an 80s diner style feel, like the aesthetic with the black and white is pleasing and nostalgic. It makes you feel a blast from the past when you slip them on, and can remind you of the good old days. Nostalgia alone makes people want to buy things, so it is no surprise how desirable these sneakers truly are. These shoes may not have a ton of design features, but they certainly do have a crisp style and will pair well with any item.

If you find a pair of these beauties at listing price, you had better snag them up. They are a hot item with many interested buyers, so even though their factory-released price is $100.00, they are not found for that price anymore.

Nike Dunk Low SE 'NY vs. NY'

$430

These streetball themed shoes were set to hit the market in 2020, but with covid cancelling all of the streetball events, their release was pushed back to August of this year. This is understandable, since the shoes are literally centered around the streetball events that everyone looks forward to each year. However, when they were finally released, they were a hit amongst the sneaker crowd. How could they not be? The vibrant orange hue of the swoosh contrasting starkly with the sage green base, interrupted only by chunks of glossy white leather, these shoes are killing it with style. Let's not forget the soles of the shoes. The translucent soles boast all of the streetball events planned for the year like a personal itinerary.

These shoes will have all of your friends drooling over your style choice, with a retail price of $250.00.

Nike Dunk Low X Off-White 'The 50' Collection

$350.00 - $1,500.00

Some people complain that with a new release of a hyped sneaker occurs, it is impossible to retain individuality, because every sneakerhead has the same pair as you. Nike is to the rescue to help you fix that problem with their Off White Dunk Low collection. Dubbed "the 50 collection", these sneakers will have 50 different variations of style. Perfect for the sneakerhead that likes to stand out while also being part of the 'in' crowd. Almost every style comes with some standard features though. So let's take a look at those.

49 out of 50 of these "Dear Summer" collaboration sneakers have a basic color combination of white and gray. The one that stands out however, has black all over, only offset by a metal gray swoosh. Every single pair from this collection has a

number plate boasting where it lies in the collection. There are two possible material combinations for these dunks depending on which pair you get. You either find leather and canvas, or hairy suede and leather. Any set you get is guaranteed to be a hit with your friends.

All colorways were released at a retail price of $180.00.

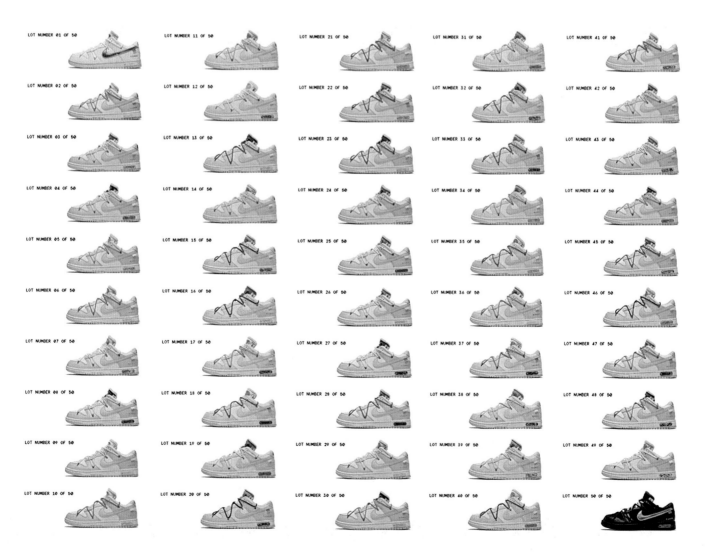

03/04/2021

Nike SB Dunk Low 'Supreme Stars'

$950.00

These are desirable sneakers that don't stay on the shelf long. It doesn't help that unlike with most of Nike's line, you can only find these retail at one place. These unique styled sneakers are only available on Supreme New York's website. Like the 50 collection mentioned above, these sneakers come in a variety of styles as well. Not quite as many as the 50 collection, but there are still a few different looks to choose from.

The 'Hyper Royale' is a white base with blue accents. Behind the cobalt blue swoosh, the white is dotted with metallic gold stars. The contrast of the blue on the white gives a crisp, clean look. The 'Mean Green' colorway has the white and the stars just like the 'Hyper Royale' one, but it's accents are a vibrant mint green. If you are wanting a more retro look, you could get the 'Black' colorway with black accents against the white base and gold stars or you could get the 'Barkroot Brown' colorway which features brown accents! Each of these sneakers also feature a metallic gold Nike logo on the tongue and a gold-plated lace charm on each shoe with the word Supreme emblazoned on it.

While retail they are $110.00, it is often hard to find them at that price. Due to them only being released in limited quantities at one location, scalpers have taken to buying them up and pricing them at a nearly 1000% increase and sometimes even more.

Nike SB Dunk Low 'What The Paul'

$450.00

Paul Rodriguez (P-Rod) is an American skateboarder who also acts, raps, and is a recording artist. He has medaled in the X Games, with 4 golds, most recently one in California in 2012. He grew up meeting celebrities and got his nickname when he was 11 from his classmates. He started skateboarding when he was 12, and was hooked from then on. Now, he collaborates with many different celebrities and brands, including Nike.

These brilliantly colored sneakers are a magnificent addition to any collection. Celebrating Paul Rodriguez, these mismatched colorways are in stark contrast with each other. Making notes of P-Rod's "Mexican Blanket" and "Stash", they also have hints of the skateboarder's usual Nike Silhouettes, and even seem to take elements from the similarly titled Jordan's "J-Rod's".

These are a pair of sneakers you would have to see in person to truly appreciate, because no picture truly does them justice. Retail price of these sneaker are $150.00. Typical resale value is at about $450.00 if you are looking to buy today.

Nike Dunk Low SP 'City Market'

$250.00

Inspired by Nike's Blue Ribbon studios (a place where Nike employees go to unleash creativity), these shoes are definitely unique. Definitely a break from the normal with most Nike sneakers, these shoes do not boast a starkly contrasting swoosh. In fact, on these shoes, the swoosh isn't the focal point at all, being translucent so as to showcase the base pattern peeking out behind it and wrapping around the heel of the shoe.

So why are these shoes so different; with their wide array of patterns and strange little additions? Why is there a small zippered pouch on the tongue, and why does it look like they used flour sacks to make these shoes? These shoes commemorate the efforts of most city markets to protect the environment, and reduce, reuse, and recycle. They also pay respect to Nike's roots in Blue Ribbon Sports.

These 'upcycled' shoes are a great addition to any showcased collection, or even to be worn if you so desire. They will definitely turn heads, and start conversations. These sneakers come with a retail price of $110.00. These don't have a high resale due to continual availability, but can still net about $250.00.

Nike Dunk High
'Notre'

$690.00

Notre is a sneaker shop found in Chicago that Nike teamed up with to release two styles of gorgeous leather and shaggy suede sneakers. These beautiful yet understated sneakers come in two colors. The "Orewood Brown" style that was released on January 21st can only be found at the Notre shop. As the name states, these are the pair with the gorgeous cool brown -almost gray- overlays.

The "Midnight Navy" version can be found on SNKRS and Stock X, and boasts a delectable midnight blue overlay that is to die for. While the Orewood brown pair have a bright white leather base, the Midnight Navy has a fossil gray leather base.

These two colors will both rock your world. At $150.00 they were reasonably priced at retail. The resell price for a pair of these sneakers is $690.00.

Nike SB Dunk High 'Carpet Company'

$250.00

These kicks were the hype of the season when the whispers of them first came out. These gorgeous microsuede accented high tops are the product of a collaboration between the Carpet Company and Nike. With a crisp white leather that is where the left and right shoes stop being identical. The right shoe stays crisp and clean with blue microsuede accents against the white leather base. The left shoe is a yellow worn-down-looking microsuede inside the blue microsuede outline. The left shoe also has some yellow tint to the white leather base. The contrast between the two looks like you are wearing the same shoe, but one looks significantly older than the other.

This collaboration had a retail price of $125.00. Not bad at all for such an in-depth design. However, resell you will have to spend $380.00 on them.

Nike Air Max 90
'Bacon'

$140.00

Released on "Air Max Day" March 26th, 2021, these sneakers display the typical Air Max 90 shape. Titled the Bacon, this sneaker is aptly named, roughly resembling the color scheme of a strip of raw bacon. This is a re-release, as the original came out in 2004. With a blinding white leather base and red and gray accents, coupled with a pink tongue and swoosh, and brown rubber accents across the shoe, these sneakers are still the desirable shoes they once were.

This iconic shoe is flying off the shelves, but hopefully won't bring the scalper frenzy to the party. Right now you can get them for $140.00 at many select retailers all over, so hopefully with a wide range of availability, there will be plenty to go around, and no need for scalpers. In fact, it looks like they can sometimes be found cheaper on sites like StockX ($109.00).

Nike Air Max 97 Swarovski 'Polar Blue'

$555.00

Daniel Swarovski became skilled in glass cutting from a young age due to being the son of a glass cutter. He grew up in Bohemia in the late 1800s. He started the Swarovski crystal business that has remained a family business since its creation in 1895. They specialize in crystal jewelry and optical instruments. The crystals they produce are to die for, and are used in many elements of fashion for their extreme clarity and shimmering beauty. Nike decided to capitalize on the popularity of the crystal in one of their latest designs.

These women's Air Maxes are not your average athletic shoe. Encrusted in Swarovski crystals, these shoes will be the shining star in your life. Glittering like a diamond on a fancy wedding ring, these sneakers are a great fashion statement while being comfortable to boot. A soft, light gray mesh is the perfect base to showcase the shine of the crystals. The normal large swoosh on the side of Nike sneakers has been miniaturized to accent the shape of the overlays perfectly.

Being as these aren't your standard Nike sneakers, of course they come at an above standard price. However, given the amount of crystals on each pair, $400.00 retail price seems very good. Resale is around $555.00.

Nike Kobe 5 Protro 'Undefeated Hall of Fame'

$250.00 - $300.00

Celebrating the life of the late Kobe Bryant, these sneakers look to his Hall of Fame induction. The gold color mesh base, and leather scaled gold overlays are accented by the blue and red swooshes that bear his three jersey numbers. The toe contains his Mamba logo, and the insole lists his accomplishments throughout his life. These shoes are high on the wishlist of sneakerheads and Kobe fans alike.

The retail price was $190.00. These now resell for about $250.00-$300.00.

Nike Waffle One *SE* '*The Whitaker Group*'

$1,500.00

A limited edition sneaker style, releasing only 500 numbered pairs, these are sure to be the eye catcher of collectors everywhere. The Whitaker Group is a non-profit organization that paired up with Nike to release a special edition Waffle One sneaker to raise money for their cause.

These shoes boast a leather upper that is covered with a large mesh cutout, bronze ankle trim and laces, a large black swoosh, rubber heel caps and a yellowed midsole. The shoes are definitely a fashion statement, and they are limited edition so they are sure to go quickly.

When they were released they were $120.00, with one pair being raffled off to help their non-profit even more. Now they are sold out, with no more being made, so people have taken to buying them on Ebay. Their limited quantities have driven up the price, with some pairs selling at close to $1,500.00. They are definitely a popular and stylish shoe.

Jordan 1 Retro High 'Trophy Room Chicago'

$1,750.00

Trophy Room is special to the Jordan line for one major reason. The founder of Trophy room is none other than Marcus Jordan, the son of Michael Jordan. Trophy room is a sneaker boutique that Marcus opened up after ending his collegiate basketball career. However, it wasn't immediately after he walked away from the court that his dream came to fruition. Initially his father refused to put up the funding for the store due to Marcus's lack of experience in running a store. However, Marcus didn't give up and teamed up with James Whitner, who owns Social Status and A Ma Maniere (two names you will also see in this book). Whitner taught Marcus the ropes, and finally Trophy Room became a reality. Now the company is teaming up with Nike on a nostalgic collaboration.

Putting a spin on the OG "Chicago" release, these sneakers reprise the white, red, and black color scheme of the Air Jordan 1s we love so much. White uppers, overlaid with red glitter, and big black Nike swooshes are sure to make you feel fresh on and off the court. The tongue displays the Nike Air logo, the translucent outsoles are dotted with red and blue stars, and the insoles are stamped with the Trophy Room insignia.

These shoes bring back the memories from back when Jordans were a new name, and everyone had to have a pair. Nowadays they are still as popular, but not for the same reasons. Back then, it was because of the endorsement and name attachment of Michael Jordan himself. Now it's because of the crazy color schemes and who doesn't want a pair of Jordans?

There was a raffle to win a free pair of these shoes at the beginning of the year, saving the winner $190.00. These sneakers have an insane resale value at $1,750.00

Jordan 4 Retro SP
'30th Anniversary Union Taupe Haze'

$625.00

Union is a contemporary clothing boutique in Los Angeles. They started in 1986 in NYC, and opened what is now their only store in Los Angeles shortly thereafter. They have the concept that states that they walk the line of fashion and function. They like to make their clothes as functional as they are stylish. They strive to stay away from the costume appearance of clothing, and opt for the more relaxed style that gets the job done while still looking good.

Union and Nike teamed up for Union's 30th anniversary to commemorate the milestone with two different styles of the Air Jordan 4. One coming in a "Desert Moss" color scheme, and the one mentioned here, the "Taupe Haze" color scheme. These sneakers are similar in structure to the previous Union x Air Jordan 4 release and they boast suede, mesh, hand-branded insignias, and pre folded tongues.

These shoes would have cost you retail $225.00. When looking to resell, you can net about $625.00 with these shoes.

Jordan 6 Retro 'Travis Scott'

$530.00

Travis Scott is a well-known rapper, and has his hand in many different things. He even has his own box of cereal. He was initially discovered by Epic Records, and published with Kanye West. Since his discovery in 2012, he quickly rose to the top of the charts, and started being recognized by major brands. He was, and still remains "the next big thing".

He teamed up with Nike to release a special edition set of Jordans in his name. These sneakers boast a "British Khaki" upper with midsoles dotted with red but mainly white. They also have red and white heel caps, a button pouch on the inner side, and crimson lettering. These shoes have the standard air cushion that Jordans have, and offer functionality and fashion. They are a high top sneaker with a thin tongue. They also don't feature the Nike swoosh, but do have the Jumpman on the heel.

These shoes are an iconic collaboration with a rapper who is well known not just for his music, but for his well-rounded interests. You can't look anywhere these days without seeing Travis Scott's name on something, and that is honestly inspiring. Wear your own inspiration for $220.00, if bought at retail. For resale you are looking at around $530.00.

Jordan 1 High OG SP Fragment x Travis Scott

$1,500.00

Yet another Jordan x Travis Scott collaboration. This time with the Jordan 1 line. These high top shoes are a simple but bold color scheme. The white base color of the shoe is accented by black overlays and blue insoles, heel caps, and soles. The typical Nike swoosh is backwards and consists of a cream color. It also displays the logo of Cactus Jack on the tongue. The heels have cool little additions with a smiley face stitched on the left, and a double lightning bolt on the right.

Coming in at $1,500.00, the value of these shoes exponentially increased when they left the store. You can also find this colorway in a low top version.

The retail price of these shoes where $150.00.

Jordan 1 High Zoom Air CMFT 'Aleali May Califia'

$225.00

Coming forward with another collaboration from her long history with Nike, Aleali May is on her third reworking of the Jordan line. These shoes scream school spirit almost with the bold colors, and shiny satin finishes. These would definitely appeal to your inner varsity teenager that is still hidden deep inside you. Teens and adults alike can jump for joy with these delightful sneakers with a brilliant emerald green base color, and striking cerulean blue overlays. The sole of the shoe is white trimmed in green, and you will also find a puffy sherpa cloud logo on the outer ankle.

Aleali definitely lets her personality shine through in all of her fashion designs. The bright colors seem to come directly from her soul, and certainly speak to ours. These sneakers retailed at $140.00. Talk about a steal to literally wear art on your feet. Resale isn't as high as some of the others, netting around $225.00.

Jordan 1 Retro High 85 'Neutral Grey'

$428.00

For the first time since 1985, these crisp, iconic sneakers will be making a return to the shelves in February of 2021. Initially Nike marketed them to be limited edition, and sold with a drawstring bag marking the edition number, but changed their mind on doing so after seeing the interest in these shoes. While it may seem like they wouldn't sell out with 23,000 pairs for sale, this design is so sleek and pairs well with any outfit, making it one of the more highly desired designs. Shortly before release, Nike removed the listing description stating there would only be 23,000 pairs released and decided to keep producing this sneaker.

So what makes this sneaker so highly sought out? The simplicity of it. Not everyone wants bold sneakers all the time. Most people want a pair that is understated to wear with everyday casual outfits. While bold is beautiful, there is something sophisticated by a monochromatic color scheme that catches the eye in a different manner. These sneakers do exactly that, with their white leather uppers, and gray accents, there are not many outfits this shoe would not compliment beautifully. Another thing that many sneaker lovers may notice is the different Air Jordan Logo. Instead of Jordan's iconic silhouette, there is a basketball with wings, the original airborne logo that represented Michael Jordan's ability to soar through the air on a dunk.

Nike released this pair with a retail price of $200.00. The resale value is more than double the retail cost coming in at $428.00.

Jordan 1 Retro High 'White University Blue Black'

$1,750.00

These shoes come in a familiar retro style with a colorway that nods to Michael Jordan's college days, hence the name "University Blue". These shoes are a wonderful blend of leather and suede, with colors that almost remind you of a crisp clear summer afternoon. With a white leather base color, the overlays are a clear sky blue in a velvety, smooth suede. The shoe is accented with black throughout, and the swoosh is black as well. As is customary with the retro line, the original logo reappears on this sneaker as well.

These sneakers are a beautiful combining of the past with today, and many are excited to get a pair of OG retro shoes. They are sure to fly off the shelves, so make sure you get yours soon. The 'University Blues' had a retail price of $170.00. However, you can garner around $430.00 on the resale.

Jordan 1 Retro High OG
'Seafoam'

$220.00

A new shoe with the retro style, these women's Jordans were just a rumor for a while. Set to release in August, these sneakers come with a brilliant white leather upper, seafoam green suede overlays, and white laces with orange trim.

These are a new design of the Retro 1s, meaning they've never been released before. However, they still have the retro silhouette, so they are considered as such. Regardless of what they are, they are an amazing shoe that look super comfortable, and cute to boot.

These sneakers will set you back only about $170.00 retail, and $220.00 resell.

Jordan 1 Retro High 'Hyper Royal Smoke Grey'

$270.00

The best part of summer is getting to show off your style more than you can in the colder months. When it is snowing, it is hard to have style when all you care about is staying warm. However, there are so many more options in the summer as layers come off and sneakers are less in danger from the harsh elements. Spring and summer clothing collections are all the rage, and Nike has the Jordans for the summer this year.

Part of the spring and summer lineup, these shoes are coming in hotter than the weather, with a refreshingly cool color palette. With royal blue suede overlaying white leather, accented by a gray swoosh, these shoes will give you a chill vibe to rock the summer with.

These icy kicks would have cost you about $170.00 retail. You can resell them for about $270.00.

Jordan 1 Retro High 'Shadow 2.0'

$218.00

In 1985, the shadow version of the OG Jordan 1s was released as a part of the original color lineup. It has now been remastered and released as the Shadow 2.0. Another steamy one for the summer lineup, these shoes flipped the original colorway of the OG Shadow. The 2.0 features a luxurious black leather background, and a supple silver suede overlay. The silver continues to accentuate the black throughout, also appearing on the heel cap and the swoosh.

These gorgeous shoes will take you to new heights with their high topped glory. $190.00 was the retail price of these sneakers. They don't net you much more when you resell them though, as they are priced currently on StockX for $208.00.

06/10/2021

Jordan 3 Retro
'A Ma Maniére'

$290.00

A Ma Maniere is an Atlanta based company that chose to work with Nike for a 2021 Retro 3 release. Together the pair designed a gorgeous woman's shoe to turn heads and keep you fashionable. These shoes have a vintage aesthetic that is coupled with beautiful gray suede overlaying a white leather base, with violet accents throughout. The soles and eyelets are yellowed slightly to add to the vintage feel of the shoe.

These shoes were released at two different times. They released in select stores on April 28th, but didn't release online until June 10th. Both places offered these sneakers for $200.00. Resale will get you about $290.00.

Jordan 4 Retro 'Shimmer'

$280.00

Around the middle of December, Nike gave a little teaser of this sneaker. However, they held out until the next fall to release this shoe. Available in women's sizing only, this shoe celebrates women providing safe space for other women, and is inspired by neutral makeup palettes.

While it draws comparison to a similar design by Off-White, who collaborated with Nike in 2020, this shoe has made some serious design changes.

Nike took a design that has been around for over 30 years and made it fresh. There are some accents throughout the sneaker, subtly breaking up the tan shimmer hue. These accents are white and silver to accent and compliment the shoe to perfection.

This shoe is available in women's sizing for somewhere in the ballpark of $190.00 depending on the retailer you go to and taxes. However, now resell price is close to $280.00.

Jordan 4 Retro 'White Oreo '

$260.00

These low topped sneakers will have you feeling fresh and fly. Similar to the high top retro Jordan 1s mentioned earlier, these have a similar white and gray colorway. However, they have one major difference, and that is that these shoes are accented by small amounts of crimson. The jumpman on the tongue and the bottom of the shoe are a bright red, adding a splash of color to the sneaker to really draw attention to the shoes.

They also have gray rubber lacestays, that look like they have inkblots on them. This subtle detail would be hard to notice if you weren't looking closely, however, it really adds to the character of the sneaker. You could find the Jordan 4 Retros in White Oreo to retail at $190.00 however the resell price is around $260.00.

Jordan 4 Retro 'Lightning'

$290.00

These shoes were limited edition when they were originally released in 2006. They were an online only sale, with a limited amount of sneakers available. These iconic shoes sold out rapidly and haven't been available since, until 2021. The release brings back the shoe that so many wanted, and so few could have. The 2006 release saw prices that many in 2006 couldn't afford, as the shoe was revered and resold like the Holy Grail. If you were one of those sneakerheads back then that wasn't able to snag the Lightning, now is your chance. These bright sneakers are draped mostly in yellow, with some dark blue-gray adding a contrast to the bright sneaker. Hints of black further compliment the yellow all wrapped up in a high top sneaker.

Feel the excitement from 2006 hit your soul and get yourself a pair of the Jordan 4 Retro Lightning shoes online for $290.00 resell today.

Jordan 4 Retro 'Taupe Haze'

$350.00

Jordan also released their own Taupe Haze retro 4 this year, and they are going to make serious waves. Sneak peeks have shown that the shoe looks cracked and worn, but don't fret because that is part of the design. Once the cracked section wears away, there will be a whole new design underneath. The taupe haze works well with the oil gray accents that are spilled throughout the shoe. The cracking throughout the shoe is subtle and very noticeable but will leave you feeling like you have a new shoe once it wears away.

If changing designs are what you are looking for, you can pick these up for around $350.00. Retail price was $200.00.

Jordan 4 Retro SP
'30th Anniversary Union Desert Moss'

$350.00

Just like the Taupe Haze mentioned above, these shoes were released in a collaboration with Union for their 30th anniversary. This retro style shoe is bolder than its counterpart, giving us serious 90s vibes.

The shoes are decked out in white mesh panels over a royal purple canvas base, with mustard yellow suede overlays and blue and dark gray checked laces.

They also have a clear top lacestay and turquoise bottom lacestay. They look like the windbreaker every elementary kid in the 90s owned all wrapped up in an awesome sneaker.

These sneakers retailed at $225.00 and they will set you back about $350.00 on the resale.

Adidas Yeezy '450'

$300.00

These top of the line shoes have been the whispers among many sneakerheads since Kanye West started showing ideas in 2019 for the next collaboration. After a long wait of tantalizing teasers, we have finally been graced with the presence of the Adidas Yeezy 450. This shoe was rumored to be called the 451, but this cloud-like shoe is dubbed the 450 instead. It hugs the feet with a sock-like fit, influenced by Steven Smith.

Many were surprised at the colorway of these shoes considering the rumors of all the design ideas that Kanye had for the potential new release. The cloud white sole with the gray athletic sock material was not what people were expecting, but they are beautiful nonetheless. So if you got yours at retail $200.00 you will be happy to know that they resale at around $300.00, so you could get a crisp hundred dollar bill if you decide to list them.

Adidas Yeezy Slide

$130.00

Slides are the term for slip on shoes that have a single band across the top that holds the shoe on the foot. These were originally debuted in 2019, and since then have been released in a variety of designs and colors.

Kanye West has toyed with the idea of many different designs of slides and other hands free shoes, but few actually see the final line to the shelves. The slides available today are named "Resin", "Desert Sand", "Bone", "Soot" and "Core".

The shoe has a solid upper, a serrated sole and is made to look like a whole one-piece slide. Inspired by the Yeezy foam rubber, these slides are a hot item that sell out fast and don't stay on the shelves long at all.

These slides are the cheapest thing you will find from Yeezy's shoe line, coming in at around $55.00 per pair retail. The toddler slides also offer a heel strap to keep them on the little ones' feet. Unlike other shoes meant for lounging, the Yeezy's don't include BOOST. This is how the price stays affordable. While this may be different in the future, it could affect the price of the shoe. However, they are reselling at prices of over $130.00, so maybe you could make some cash if you bought them at retail.

"Yeezy Slides" is an umbrella term for all of the models, but there is a possible name adjustment with these and future models such as the Yeezy 450 Slides to help differentiate between each new release. The new colorways are hitting the shelves, so grab yours while you can.

03/17/2021

Adidas Forum Low Bad Bunny

$600.00

Bad Bunny is a Puerto Rican/Dominican Rapper that has a reggaeton and trap music style. However, his style is honestly more eclectic than that as he is a huge fan of collaborating with other artists, both in music and fashion. He made waves in 2020, being the first Latin artist on the cover of a Rolling Stones magazine, and performed at the Super Bowl halftime show alongside J-Lo and Shakira.

But he isn't just making waves in music, he is making waves in fashion as well. He has collaborated with Adidas for the third time to make a new addition to his Forum Low line. These sneakers are an all-black version of the Forum Low with some typical features you find with his other versions. First it still has the double tongue that the style is known for. It also has the buckle and lock strap on the ankle. The entire shoe is black, aside from the eye logo and the lime green lace tips.

These are definitely a pair of sneakers to get hyped for, and for good reason. They are completely iconic due to the collaboration alone, and the unique design makes them even better. They retailed at $160.00. The resale value is insane though, at almost $600.00, these are super popular due to limited quantities when they are released.

Adidas Superstar Bape ABC Camo Green

$300.00

Adidas is coming up on the 50th anniversary of the Superstar Original. To celebrate, BAPE, who has done many collaborations with Adidas, has put a spin on the silhouette that the company, which is a staple of street fashion in Japan, has helped with many times before. This year, the sneaker will have two different color schemes. The black and white classic, and a colorful camo style with a mismatched scheme.

The shoes have dual designs. The left side is branded with the Adidas Stripes, and the left has the Bape's logo, which is a shooting star. The tongues also have the branding of each company coinciding with the side of the shoe the brands are on (Adidas left, Bape right).

These two companies have teamed up on previous iterations of the Superstar previously. In fact, the first one came out in 2003, and in 2011 and 2015, two more designs were released. BAPE is actually fairly well known for their personal "knock off" brand of the Superstar, titled the "Skull-Sta".

These shoes retailed for $170.00. Some versions of the shoe resell for over $300.00.

Adidas NMD Hu
'Pharrell Williams' Cream

$540.00

Pharrell Williams is a very popular pop music artist, known most widely for his viral hit single "Happy" and being married to Chrissy Teigan. He is lesser known for being a fashion designer, and also a record producer. He has teamed up with Adidas a few times to create some really awesome shoes.

This year, Williams and Adidas have created a line of shoes called the NMD Hu. They come in a wide variety of colors and are being released throughout the year. They are BOOST enhanced shoes, and are the pinnacle of comfort. Featuring a primeknit upper and a foam sole, these shoes are the epitome of style and comfort. The shoes also come with plastic lace holders, a heel overlay and EVA plugs on the midsole.

These shoes, in all of their colors and designs, bring comfort and style together. A pair would have cost you $220.00 retail. The cream color of these shoes resells at $540.00, while the rest are pretty close to retail.

New Balance 2002R
Salehe Bembury 'Water Be The Guide'

$250.00

Salehe Bembury is a crossover footwear artist, who used to design for Kanye West on his Yeezy line. He is now vice president of sneakers and men's footwear at Versace. There is not a lot known about him at this point, but most of what is known about him is his history in shoe design. He started at Payless, and worked his way up. This year he teamed up with New Balance to bring a unique look to the brand, and really put the name of fashion out there with a New Balance tag.

Breathable material meets comfy and cozy in this collaboration, and nature meets humanity as well. These shoes are beautiful, and look like a pair of shoes a forest nymph would wear. The iconic New Balance shape and structure remains, but the colorway is where these shoes stand out. With a bright cyan shaggy suede overlays and mesh cutouts in the shoe accented by an orange tongue and mini N logo on the top of the shoe, these shoes will make you want to frolic in a mossy glade. Even the logo screams nature, looking like a grassy knoll with dark green suede outlined in neon green stitched as a trim.

Retail for a pair of these sneakers would have set you back $150.00. However, they resell for around $250.00.

New Balance 237
'Casablanca'

$260.00

Casablanca is an up and coming fashion company that started in France just before the lockdown. It was founded as homage to the owner of the company's heritage, and it is more than just a brand. It is a community and a lifestyle. The designs are brought to life in the colors and hues that are chosen for each piece. Recently they have teamed up with New Balance to create some sneakers. In fact, this season's release is their third collaboration.

The past two collaborations have been the 327 silhouettes that New Balance is famous for. They were meant for casual wear, and monogrammed with Casablancas signature. There are a few other similarities between the different releases, but the biggest difference is that this year they are designing the newer New Balance 237 sneakers instead of the 327. This season's collaboration is also the cleanest color palette used of the designs.

With a white base, and mint green and baby pink accents, you would think the color scheme alone would make you jump for these shoes. However, instead of just having straight color accents, these shoes have a pattern on them. And not just stripes or lines, an intricate pattern of diamond like shapes intertwining with little links locking in the center of each one. The tongue also has a design to look like a flower going up the middle under the white, gold-tipped, laces. The enlarged N is white shadowed by baby pink, and the soles are mint green.

If you are looking for a unique shoe with an intricate pattern rather than just your standard solid color overlays, then this is the shoe for you. Retail price of these sneakers were $150.00 with resell going as high as $260.00.

New Balance 991
'Patta'

$540.00

Patta is a duch company that specializes in footwear. Recently they teamed up with Nike to celebrate the 20th anniversary of the 991 New Balance sneaker. With a pistachio green mesh base, and tan overlays dressed in suede and leather, it is a neutral color palette to pair well with many different looks. The warm tones will bring a bit of spice to your outfit, and the comfort will keep you rocking all day long. On the lateral heel of the sneaker you will find the Patta branding.

$220.00 retail. They resell at $540.00, which is more than double the initial retail price.

Reebok Zig Kinetica II 'Brain Dead'

$125.00

You may be wondering who Brain Dead is, and if this is an insult to those who are on life support. Rest your soul, because Brain Dead refers to the group of creative individuals from around the world with the soul purpose to disrupt the world with their art. They are a nod to post punk underground vibes. It is not one person, it is the collection of the void.

Brain Dead is not particularly new to collaborating with Reebok. In fact, this is their third collaboration. The Zig Kinetica II is out in two glorious cover options. This Zig silhouette is a great sized canvas for the collaborative to get creative on without losing functionality.

The shoe features Reebok's Floatride Fuel comfortable cushioning and the Zig Energy Shell. This means that the shoe will support your foot and return energy to the person wearing it as they walk. These shoes are designed for sports, and made to help reduce injury to the joints by dispersing the force that you drive into your feet with every step, and placing it over a wider surface area.

Let's talk about the colorways of the two sneakers shall we? The first one is a light gray suede with white accents. The middle of the upper of the shoe is a white mesh with yellow wavy lines. The midsole looks like a sunset with hues of crimson and sunflower, followed by white streaked with cyan. The 'laces' of the shoe are an adjustable bungee cord that allows you to quickly put on these shoes and get moving.

These shoes are made for running, jumping, you name it. If you want some shoes that will keep your feet in as good of shape as you want to be in, these are the shoes for you. You can find them online and at select shoe retailers for $160.00, but you may be better off buying them on the resell from someone else, as they are not super popular and are actually cheaper. They resell for about $125.00 right now.

A Bathing Ape 'Court Sta'

$1,800.00

Bape is releasing their own line of shoes called the Court Sta this year. While they are known for collaborations, they are making waves, and raising eyebrows, with their newest release. The Court Sta takes heavy inspiration from the Air Jordan 1, and will come in both low and high tops.

The sneaker has three different color iterations. The high tops are black and gray and the low tops are two different color schemes.

The first is white and gray, and the second will be sail, gray and purple. The overlays of all of the shoes have the signature camouflage print on the overlays, and the zig zag star logo that is associated with the company.

These sneakers ranged from $305.00 to $319.00 when retail. If you want to get your hands on them, you will have to hit the bank and withdraw some money since they resell for around $1,800.00.

CONCLUSION

2021 was the year for sneaker releases. Nike alone released a ton of new styles to their already epic lines. Don't even get me started on the 50 collection, or we could be here all day. This was the year for sneakerheads to rejoice, as there are so many options to choose from. Jordans came out hot this year, especially with their retros. New Balance, and Reebok also had some cool debuts as well. Adidas had some good collaborations, and A Bathing Ape is making a name for themselves.

No matter your style, 2021 probably had a release that caught your eye. Possibly several for that matter. I know I have a few that I really want! The Nike Dunk Low 50 collection is full of amazing styles and I can't choose which one I want! Might as well get one of each.

Another amazing thing about 2021 is all of the companies that raffled off a pair of their new shoes and donated the proceeds to charity. A great way to show a sense of community, and show off the new releases! While just selling one pair of shoes will only get the price of the shoe back, a raffle can potentially make thousands of dollars, and every penny counts when it goes to helping others.

Whether you are an avid sneaker wearer, or a sneaker collector, everyone can agree that these styles are something to get your hands on in a hurry. Especially the limited edition sneakers that are only available in certain amounts. Go forth, and spread the joy of fashion and sneakers with the knowledge on what to look for.

REFERENCES

Air Jordan 1 85 Neutral Grey BQ4422-100 2021 Release Date - SBD. (2021 January 27). Sneaker Bar Detroit. https://sneakerbardetroit.com/air-jordan-1-85-neutral-grey-bq4422-100-2021-release-date/

Air Jordan 1 Archives. (n.d.). Nice Kicks. https://www.nicekicks.com/air-jordans/air-jordan-1/

Air Jordan 1 Hyper Royal 555088-402 Release Date - SBD. (2021 April 2). Sneaker Bar Detroit. https://sneakerbardetroit.com/air-jordan-1-hyper-royal-light-smoke-grey-white-555088-402-release-date/

Air Jordan 1 University Blue 555088-134 Release Date - SBD. (2021 February 11). Sneaker Bar Detroit. https://sneakerbardetroit.com/air-jordan-1-white-university-blue-black-555088-134-release-date/

Aleali May Air Jordan 1 Zoom CMFT "Califia" Store List | SneakerNews.com. (2021 April 13). Sneaker News. https://sneakernews.com/2021/04/13/aleali-may-air-jordan-1-califia-dj1199-400-release-date/

Brain Dead Reebok Zig Kinetica II S23890 S23891 Release Date - SBD. (2021 April 12). Sneaker Bar Detroit. https://sneakerbardetroit.com/brain-dead-reebok-zig-kinetica-ii-s23890-s23891-release-date/

Brain Dead-Los Angeles. (n.d.). Clothing and Home Goods in Los Angeles - Virgil Normal. https://www.virgilnormal.com/collections/brain-dead-east-side-los-angeles

Britannica. (2018). Nike, Inc. | History & Facts. In Encyclopædia Britannica. https://www.britannica.com/topic/Nike-Inc

Deng, V., & Deng, V. (2021 May 3). Jordan brand gives its classic "shadow" colorway an update on the upcoming Air Jordan 1 High release. Footwear News. https://footwearnews.com/2021/shop/sneakers-deals/air-jordan-1-high-shadow-2-0-release-info-1203136977/

DQM Nike Air Max 90 Bacon CU1816-100 2021 Release Date - SBD. (2021 March 5). Sneaker Bar Detroit. https://sneakerbardetroit.com/dqm-nike-air-max-90-bacon-release-date/

Michael, P. (2021 July 30). This kids-exclusive Nike Dunk Low arrives August 25th. HOUSE OF HEAT. https://houseofheat.co/nike/nike-dunk-low-gs-white-royal-red-cw1590-104-release-date/

Nike Air Max. (2020 February 26). Wikipedia. https://en.wikipedia.org/wiki/Nike_Air_Max

Nike Dunk Low City Market DA6125-900 Release Date - SBD. (2021 February 18). Sneaker Bar Detroit. https://sneakerbardetroit.com/nike-dunk-low-da6125-900-release-date/

Nike Dunk Low Retro Black White 2021 Release Date | SneakerNews.com. (2020 December 1). Sneaker News. https://sneakernews.com/2020/12/01/nike-dunk-low-retro-black-white-2021-release-date/

Notre Nike Dunk High 2021 Release Date. (2021 January 14). Sneaker Bar Detroit. https://sneakerbardetroit.com/notre-nike-dunk-high-release-date/

Sawyer, J. (2021a January 22). Where to buy the Nike SB Dunk Low "Street Hawker" today. Highsnobiety. https://www.highsnobiety.com/p/nike-sb-dunk-low-street-hawker-release-date-price/

Sawyer, J. (2021b May 14). UNDEFEATED x Nike Kobe 5 Protro "Hall of Fame": SNKRS release info. Highsnobiety. https://www.highsnobiety.com/p/undefeated-nike-kobe-5-protro-hall-of-fame-release-date-price/

Sawyer, J. (2021c August 10). Off-WhiteTM x Nike Dunk Low "Dear Summer": How to buy. Highsnobiety. https://www.highsnobiety.com/p/off-white-nike-dunk-low-dear-summer-release-date-price/

Supreme Nike SB Dunk Low Stars Release Date. (2021 March 1). Sneaker Bar Detroit. https://sneakerbardetroit.com/supreme-nike-sb-dunk-low-dh3228-100-dh3228-101-dh3228-102-dh3228-103-release-date/

Swarovski x Nike Air Max 97 "Polar Blue" Official Images. (2021 March 19). Sneaker News. https://sneakernews.com/2021/03/19/nike-air-max-97-swarovski-polar-blue-dh2504-001/

SCAN ME

Because We Care About
Our Readers.

Golden Lion Publications

Made in the USA
Las Vegas, NV
11 December 2022

61984719R00059